Prepping 101 The Ultimate Quick Start Crash Course

An Introduction to Disaster and Emergency Preparedness and How to Start Prepping for Beginners

Steve Rayder

www.southshorepublications.com

ISBN-13: 978-1514243916

ISBN-10: 1514243911

CONTENTS

Introduction

So you're interested in making emergency and disaster preparedness plans but you need some advice on getting started? Well, I have been a Prepper for a number of years now and written several books on preparedness and survival topics. In this short, information packed book I'm going to condense down what I have learned to give you a quick start guide to prepping.

The Reality of Prepping

Before we start I just want to mention something about the common perception of Prepping and Preppers. There are shows out there about Prepping that make us look like raving lunatics with a bad case of paranoia and a very overactive imagination. This is not the case for most Preppers. Sure, there are a few people who are a bit nuts that also prep, but this is not the majority I assure you. Most Preppers are just people who know they should be able to take care of themselves and their families if anything were to go wrong.

There are a whole range of disaster scenarios that could cause us and our families to be plunged into a life or death situation with almost no notice. Some of these scenarios come in the form of natural disasters, some in the form of pandemics and others in the form of manmade weapons, rioting or financial collapse. Because of all of these threats we face, it really does pay to be prepared and it will give you wonderful peace of mind.

Types of Prepper

There are different Preppers who see the likelihood of different disasters being higher than others so they prep fairly specifically for that exact eventuality. EMP specialist Preppers for example will ensure they have backup electronics stored in homemade foil Faraday cages. Or you could just keep general supplies that will cover almost any eventuality. Being generally prepared for a situation where a lack of food and water would occur along with potential relocation is generally considered to be the standard level of preparedness.

On a lighter note, the survival and preparedness community is a great place to be. There are many groups and forums out there full of like-minded people that you can connect with and discuss ideas with. It's not only a good idea to get prepared it's also a lot of fun and it makes a great hobby. It even gives us a good excuse to buy loads of really swish bits of survival gear and who doesn't like doing that?

Our Ancestors; the Original Preppers

Being prepared for an extended survival situation isn't a new idea. In fact it's one of the oldest ideas in the world. Thousands of years ago, our ancestors wouldn't just pop-down the shop and buy whatever food they wanted for the next week. They would have supplies in the form of grain and preserved fruit and vegetables, so that if anything went wrong, they could take care of themselves. Even in the last 200 years or so people would make their own provisions and have long term supplies of foods in storage. The idea of only keeping enough food for a week or two is a very new one.

Today's society seems to be one of surety and entitlement. People today just seem to take everything for granted and think that there will always be a shop to go to if they need anything. This is the exact reason why the Prepping movement has gained so much steam in recent years, because more and more people are noticing this change and they have realized how venerable it makes us.

You shouldn't count on other people for your basic, essential living requirements. You should always have enough food and water to see you through if anything were to happen to either of these things. This point is proved when natural disasters occur and people have no choice but to flock to dirty overcrowded camps to receive handouts in order to survive.

I don't know about you but I think most people would prefer to be able to look after themselves and their own family rather than relying on other people to come and save you. Of course, if the disaster is big enough, that help may not come for a long time. So we should all be ready for these eventualities. Your life, and your families lives may depend on it one day.

Stages of a Disaster

If a large scale disaster were to occur, such as a solar flare hitting the earth for example, there would be a few distinct stages that are common to many scenarios. Stage 1 is just after the disaster strikes where everyone is friendly and pulling together to help. Stage 2 is just four hours in and this is where people start turning nasty and thinking about their own survival once the reality has sunk in. Stage 3 is after about 2 weeks when people are dehydrating and starving due to the lack of provisions and the tap water not running anymore. Then Stage 4 is the ensuing WROL (Without Role of Law) period in which people are utterly desperate and even good people will take what they can from others in order to survive.

So you need to be prepared for this if you are concerned about these kinds of large scale disasters. The major concerns are water, food, shelter, security and communication. All of which I will be covering in this book and much more.

Potential Causes of Disaster

It's easy to feel safe in modern society and think that nothing will go wrong. Since you're new to Prepping, I wanted to kick things off by going over some of the things that could cause the potential end of the world as we know it. With the amount of things that could go wrong, it's a wonder that not everyone is preparing for them to be honest.

The Obvious Dangers

Now there are the obvious things that you may want to prepare for such as common natural disasters, but there are far worse and more threatening things out there. That's what I'm going to discuss in this chapter. This isn't just a chapter about weird conspiracy theories that will probably never happen. This stuff is actually possible.

Pandemics

Pandemics are a real cause for concern and something that we have been hearing a lot about over the past few years. New and deadly diseases are appearing faster than ever before. Some believe most of them to be man-made, but wherever they come from, they pose a real threat. Many of the most contagious new diseases have also been weaponized, so if a war breaks out they may be even be purposely released into the population.

Super Volcanoes

We all know what a volcano does when it erupts, we're talking massive damage to the surrounding area. Super volcanoes however are about a million times more powerful. If one of these things were to go off, it would definitely be the end of civilization as we know it. There are 6 super volcanoes on earth so let's hope one doesn't decide to go off any time soon and if it does, well at least will be prepared as best we can!

Solar Flares and Global Warming

Solar flares or solar storms are another big concern. This is basically the sun spewing out a huge electromagnetic pulse or EMP. There is practically no warning as these things will reach us in minutes. They have hit earth before and caused whole telephone wire systems to burst into flames. If one were to hit today in the right spot it would have the potential to knock out the entire electrical grid of any country with ease. Not only this, but Nuclear weapons have a very similar effect and also give off massive EMPs. I have actually written a whole book dedicated to this topic as it's pretty darn interesting.

Global warming is another huge threat to our way of life and the very existence of humanity. Most people think this is due to fossil fuels and emissions, and that turning off lights or getting an electric car is the answer. In fact it's mainly due to modern animal agriculture and the meat industry so you're much better off going vegetarian if you want to help stop global warming!

Global warming and climate change pose threats in a number of ways. Firstly, as you have probably heard, bees have been dying by the millions since 2006 and they are decreasing in number every year. This causes serious issues with the pollination of crops all over the world. There are about 30,000 other species of living creature going extinct every year, which is faster than at any other point in recorded history. This is causing huge changes to ecosystems and could have potentially catastrophic implications.

Gas Deposits

Some scientists believe that there are massive subterranean methane gas deposits that are in danger of melting due to climate change. If this is true then when they are released into the atmosphere global warming would be increased at a massive rate causing us even more problems.

War

War, or more specifically nuclear war, is also a distinct possibility. The most likely countries to launch nuclear weapons at each other are the United States and Russia but this would have massive implications for people the world over.

Financial Collapse

There is also financial breakdowns that could cause the structure of society to fall flat on its face in a matter of hours. If a complete financial breakdown were to occur and currency was made useless, chaos would descend on the population immediately with everyone looting and taking whatever they could find.

There are other risks such as asteroids and massive tsunamis, the Oxford University even released a study that listed artificial intelligence as the most likely cause for the apocalypse at 10% probability. However I think what I have mentioned in this chapter are the main concerns for most people. So hopefully now you have a better idea of why people do get prepared for one of these eventualities to happen. Now let's talk about exactly how to prepare.

The Basics

It's very easy to get started out in the Prepping world and begin to get the things together that will enable you to survive through an extended disaster situation. Of course there are many more things to think about and consider than what I am going to mention in this chapter, but to begin with, the first thing I would tell any budding Prepper to do is to get some decent food, water, basic hygiene and medical supplies together.

Water

Let's talk about water to begin with. Most people don't realize just how much water they really use on a daily basis. After washing yourself, you dishes and your clothing, flushing the toilet multiple times, drinking, brushing your teeth and cooking with it, you will have used a lot more than you think. So, you should always keep a backup supply of water on standby.

This is good to have anyway, even if you're not preparing for a large scale disaster. There are always possibilities of your pipes freezing or a water pipe bursting near you and leaving you without water for a few days. If this happens, everyone in your area will be heading out to the shops and buying up all of the bottled water.

In a survival situation you will need 2 gallons of water a day for general use if you're careful with it. It's up to you exactly how much you store. You may have a river running through your back garden, in which case you don't have to worry so much about water storage for example. But as a rule I would store 60 gallons per person for every month that you're planning for.

You don't have to go out and buy huge amounts of bottled spring water, you just need to get some containers and fill them with tap water. You could use empty drink bottles for this and just stack them up or you can buy large specialist containers to make things easier. You will need to boil the tap water when it comes to drinking it if you have left it for a while however. Or you can filter it without using heat, which I will talk about in the next chapter.

Food

Next, food supplies. The very basic things I would tell you to get in order to get you started out are rice and beans. Get big bags of both and start creating a stockpile. Rice and beans may not sound like the most exciting thing ever, but it does sustain life. You can supplement this with some canned goods and some other items which I will go into in more detail in the next chapter.

Medicine and Sanitation

The basic medical supplies that you should have in your home at all times are antiseptic fluid and a range of dressings and bandages. You should also keep backup supplies of painkillers and any other medications you may specifically require.

You should also keep a fairly large stock of toilet roll. This is very commonly overlooked but it's essential. If you run out then you are going to have to start using rags or ripping up your clothes. Also you should have some spare toothpaste and soap for keeping up your personal hygiene.

Lighting

You should also keep a form of lighting. As a minimum I would say a wind up flashlight is a great item to have and it's always worth keeping some candles and some spare lighters with your supplies.

That about covers it for the basics, the food and water is the main thing you should start getting together as soon as possible. These things alone will give you a big advantage over everyone else considering most people won't be able to last more than a week when the water goes off.

Getting More Advanced

So, after you have your basic supplies together you can start to think about some more advanced options. Firstly, let's talk about the other options you have for water storage and purification.

Water

I'm a big fan of sustainable things rather than single use. Having large stockpiles of water is great and will give you a massive advantage, but realistically you're only going to be able to comfortably store enough for a few months in most homes. So setting up a water collection system in advance will be a huge help.

The best way to gather water in my opinion is to set up a series of water butts in your garden. Obviously people living in apartments can't really do this but if you have a garden I would very highly recommend it. This will provide you will a fairly consistent supply of water that you can use to re-fill your used containers.

As I mentioned, you can boil water to make it safe to drink but if you're drinking rain water that you have collected you will also need to filter it first. There are a number of water filters available online or you can make your own crude water filter from household materials just to remove any floating sediment and dirt. Then you can boil it for a few minutes and it will be safe to drink.

Of course boiling water in a disaster situation likely means making a fire. As the gas and electricity will most likely be down, this will involve finding wood or other flammable items which will probably be in short supply unless you live in a remote location with a lot of trees about. Gas camping stoves are an option, but the gas won't last long under heavy daily use unless you have a lot of spare canisters on standby.

Another option to purify water without the use of heat is to get some water purification tablets. Again, these won't last for long unless you have large amounts. So, what's the best option?

In my opinion, one of the best things you can buy as a Prepper is a Berkey water filter. These things can make pretty much anything safe to drink without any form of power or heat, they just use gravity. You can even use them to purify lake or pool water. Buying one of these and a few replacement filters will enable you to purify water for a very long time easily. You can also use these on a day to day basis in your home to remove the Fluoride and all of the other chemicals that are in tap water such as the Ammonia that they use to flush the pipes through.

Food

It's best to supplement your rice and beans with some other foods to make things a bit more interesting and to maintain optimum health. Sugar and salt are great items to stockpile and will last for a long time. Also, keep some spices and flavorings. Just grab some when you're next shopping and just keep them with your supplies.

Canned food such as fruit is great to have and will provide you with some foods that are higher in sugar. You can also buy MREs which stands for Meals Ready to Eat. They are military style meals that you can eat straight from the bag and they last for years. They don't taste great though to be honest.

Medical Supplies

If you want to get more advanced with your medical supplies there are some great items that you can get to help with more serious injuries. The SWAT-T Tourniquet will enable you to reduce the blood flow to an extremity and help stop excessive bleeding. Also the Quikclot Sport 50 Gram can be used instead of a standard dressing and the enzyme it contains will cause wounds to clot and stop bleeding much faster. These both make fantastic additions to a first aid kit and will allow you to treat much more serious wounds and potentially save a life.

Bugging In and Bugging Out

You have may have heard these two terms if you have looked into Prepping as they are very common expressions in the Prepping world. They basically refer to either staying in your home and staying put for the long haul, or getting out of town and heading into a more rural area.

Bugging Out

Bugging out is what a lot of Preppers will be intending to do. There are rivers where you can gather water and fish, there's wild animals to trap or hunt too so it may seem like the obvious choice. They intend to go back to a simpler time and live off the land again. The problem with this is that when food and water is in short supply, the vast majority of people will instantly think that the best place to find more is out in the wild. Many experts predict these mass migrations of millions of people from cities and towns into woodland areas if a widespread disaster were to occur.

So very quickly, anyone out there will be hunting all of the wildlife and fishing the lakes and the rivers causing a massive and sudden decline of all animals, birds and fish. There will not be enough to feed the whole population without modern farming methods, so even in the wild, hunting with guns and traps, people will starve.

Also when bugging out, you expose yourself to the elements. Exposure from excessive heat witch limited clean water, or from low temperatures and wet conditions is the fastest way to put your life at risk in a survival situation.

The other risk you run comes from other survivors. Like I said in the introduction, after just 4 hours people will begin looting at thinking about their own survival. If you have supplies and you're bugging out with them, other people who aren't prepared and have little or no survival supplies will try and take them from you if they can. This may sound dramatic but in the chaos that would ensue, people will do anything to protect and feed their families. This includes using violence to take what they need from other people that have more than them.

So bugging out actually has many obvious and immediate disadvantages. Even the best bug out plans can go wrong. For example, some people have reinforced bug out vehicles, but what happens if the roads become blocked by fallen trees or impassable debris? Even when you get to your bug out location, there will be other people wondering into whatever area you go to before long. These people may be armed or moving in armed groups.

Bugging In

The safest option is to bug in and keep enough supplies to maintain you and your family for an extended period of time. Of course, by doing this you may still come under attack from people who want to take your supplies, but it's much easier to defend yourself in your home than it is to defend yourself out in the open.

You can keep far more supplies in your home than you can take with you out on the road meaning you will be able to survive for longer. Also the comforts of home such as having a real bed and a proper roof over your head will be a big morale booster compared to those people who are surviving in the wild. Camping or building a survival shelter might sound fun, but after a week you will be probably utterly sick of it and missing home.

That being said, there are some situations where you can't stay in your home. In some disaster scenarios there is the potential for your home or the area you live in to be destroyed or made inhabitable. These scenarios include flooding, hurricanes, fires and maybe even nuclear fallout.

So in some cases you will need to bug out. It's best to be prepared for both scenarios just in case. So over the next two chapters I will cover what you need to do to get yourself ready for both bugging in and staying put and getting out in a hurry.

Bugging In and Home Defense

Now obviously for bugging in you will need provisions, but we have already covered that. In this chapter I will go over everything else you should consider when getting ready to bug in for the long haul.

Neighbors and Community

A big consideration when considering your bugging in plans are your neighbors. In a WROL situation, you can form a neighborhood support group with the people around you. This is much harder to do on the road as you won't know the people you are bumping into and many of them will most likely treat you as being hostile right away. You neighbors are far less likely to do this.

Some people may not get on with their neighbors but there is safety in numbers and it's much better than trying to go it alone seeing as you may need to defend yourself at some point. If you have group of people who are all willing to work as a group to defend your area from potential attackers you will be in a much better position.

Working with your neighbors has more than just defensive benefits. You can also share knowledge. Maybe one of your neighbors is a shortwave radio hobbyist and he can provide you with communications with other countries. Another neighbor may have a solar panel that you can use to power that radio when the grid goes down. So by coming together you can form a much more functional group with shared expertise in different areas.

You can also barter with them for supplies that you need. Or set up trade with other communities around you. If you do decide to bug out then you will lose this local support system.

Sanitation

Sanitation is another concern for those of us who are intending to bug in. In a situation of a magnitude we are discussing, all of the utilities we take for granted would stop working. People commonly think of electricity and gas but many people fail to consider sewage.

The amount of humans living in cities and towns with no sewage would cause major sanitation issues and health risks. Your toilet will still flush if you pour a bucket of water down the bowl but who has all of that water to waste in a disaster situation?

Latrines are the most likely solution to this problem but I expect some people will still just throw their waste out onto the street or down the drains that will quickly become blocked with no maintenance. So use the toilet if you have the water to spare, if not then you're going to have to dig a latrine.

You can wash with very small amounts of water and you should keep spare soap, shampoo and tooth paste. This is something a lot of people forget when getting their survival supplies together. If you keep enough of these items you will most likely be able to trade them as they will be considered a real luxury before long.

Home Defense

You should also think about how you would defend your home in a bug in situation. This depends on the type of properly you live in along with the layout and the surrounding area. So you will have to consider the implications of these things carefully.

The most obvious thing to consider is securing your home against intruders. In my previous book about home defense I recommended two great products to look at for securing your external doors called the OnGARD and the Nightlock door braces. Both are great for securing exterior doors such and preventing intruders from breaking in via your front and back door.

For interior doors, you're not going to be able to secure them quite as well as your external doors but the Buddybar Door Jammers are great for buying you some extra time by jamming a door shut if someone does get inside. There are cheaper versions of the product available but they aren't as strong and they are more liable to just slip out of the way.

The other obvious way of protecting your home is by using weaponry, which I will go into later on in the book. But one thing that will give you a huge advantage if it does come to combat is night vision googles. You have to remember that with the grid down in most scenarios, there will be very little light at night, even in towns and cities. If an intruder want's to loot your house under the cover of darkness, they will be doing so by moonlight alone unless they want to use a flashlight and stand out like a sore thumb. So the night vision will give you a distinct advantage.

The only problem is they are fairly pricey. Something like Yukon NV Goggles are a really pro bit of kit, but they are pretty expensive. Although these will allow you to see with fairly normal depth perception even at close quarters. Or you could go for something a lot more affordable like the Polaris Explorer Monocular. This will basically allow you to use it like night vision binoculars and see what's going on around your home at night but it can't be used in close quarters due to the magnification.

Bugging Out and Bug out Bags

So we have covered why you may want or need to bug out. In order to do this you will need to carry your supplies and tools with you in an organized way. Realistically if you're planning on bugging in and only leaving when you absolutely have to, the likelihood that you will be leaving a rush is very high. So the best way to be ready for this is to have a bug out bag ready to go at a moment's notice.

You can even keep your bugout bag in your car so all you have to do is jump in and drive and you will have your supplies with you. This also means that if you're out and about when the disaster strikes, you will have everything you need to increase your chances of survival with you at all times.

Choosing a Bag

So first you will need to get yourself a bag to use for bugging out. A standard bag won't be big enough but hiking and camping backpacks work well. Tactical bags are the most functional due to their Molle system that allows you to attach various items and Molle compatible pouches to extend the capacity of the bag.

I personally use the Condor Venture. Which is absolutely fantastic and I would highly recommend it because of its great design and handy features. Its entire main section can be un-zipped right to be bottom of the bag and all of the way around making for easy packing and easy access to items in the bottom of the bag without unpacking it entirely.

This bag is also incredibly comfortable which is something you need to keep in mind. The Venture has a rigid back board with padding on top which is something you should look for. This means the bag always keeps its shape for maximum comfort and no objects inside the bag will ever poke you in the back.

Another thing you should consider, which the Venture has, is chest and waist straps that will help support the bag when walking long distances. The Venture has a removable waist strap which is very handy meaning you have the option of only using it when you need it, then when you don't it doesn't get in the way. This also means that you can use the waist strap as a separate utility belt and add Molle Pouches to it which is very handy.

No matter what bag you choose, you should go for something that is at least 30 liters as you will need to carry a lot with you. So, what should you keep in your bag to unsure you have the best chance of survival as possible?

Blades and Cutting Tools

A good quality multi-tool is something you should have with you due to its wide range of uses. It's worth paying for high quality as the cheaper tools are prone to breaking and bending. I personally have the Leatherman Wave because I believe it's one of the best, high-end multitool models out there. Incredible quality and very strong. I pretty much use my Leatherman on a daily basis so it's worth getting a good one. Obviously a multitool will have knives on it, but this shouldn't be your primary blade.

A good quality full tang knife should be high on your list of priorities as they have a range of applications and are probably one of the most useful bits of kit you will have at your disposal.

You should also be carrying a folding saw and a fold up entrenching tool. For my saw I went for the Bacho Laplander and can vouch for its quality and fantastic cutting ability. This is great for shelter building and fire wood cutting. It's very compact when it is folded away, so fits nicely into a bug out bag. Folding entrenching tools like the Draper or the SOG are very cheap and will come in handy with shelter building, fire pits and latrines.

Shelter

Keeping a tarpaulin in your bag will give you a quick and easy way of throwing up a shelter without having to make one. As long as you can tie some cord between two trees and pin or weigh the tarp down then you will have something to shelter you from the elements. A hammock works well under a suspended tarp to keep you off of the cold wet ground and is a popular choice for many survivalists. You can go for something very lightweight and simple like the Grand Trunk Ultralight or something a bit more advanced with a mosquito net like the Grand Trunk Skeeter Beeter Pro.

Foil space blankets are great items that can save lives in cold conditions. They can also be used as a heat reflector for a fire, a small makeshift tarp, a ground sheet, a large signaling mirror and to keep you cool among other things. So they are a great item to have.

Sleeping bags will add to the carry weight of your bag considerably. So unless you live in a very cold area, I would go for a military issue wool blanket instead. Wool blankets will keep you warm even when they are damp, are fire retardant and they are more compact and lightweight than a sleeping bag.

Cordage

You should also keep some paracord in your bag as cordage is useful for a whole range of things. If you haven't heard of Paracord, it's the same thing used in parachutes and is very strong. It's thinner and therefore lighter than standard rope. It also has seven thinner strands inside it that you can remove as use for more delicate work and for things such as fishing lines. The standard that most Preppers use is 550 Paracord.

Fire Lighting

Another thing that you have to keep on you is fire lighting equipment. Fires are obviously essential for keeping warm, cooking and boiling drinking water. Fire's also have a range of other uses which I go into in more detail in my book dedicated to fire.

It's best to keep a couple of lighters as they are the easiest and quickest way of getting a fire lit. However it's always best to carry a more long term method of fire lighting such as a ferro rod. If you have never heard of a ferro rod, they are basically a hard metallic cylinder that when scraped with the back of a knife or something similar, will give off very hot sparks that are enough to ignite most fine tinder. They will last for much longer than a lighter so they provide you with both a backup fire starting method and a long term solution.

Eating and Drinking

You will want to get a good quality solid steel canteen with no coating to keep in your bug out bag too. Klean Kanteen are a good choice. This will allow you to boil water to make it safe to drink in the canteen itself as you can place it straight on the fire. To go with this you will also want to get mess tins. A stainless steel mug is also very handy for drinking out of and brewing up natural teas. Finally, a set of stainless steel cutlery is very handy indeed.

It may not always be possible or practical to start a fire to boil water for drinking, so you should keep some water purification tablets in your bag for this eventuality.

Medical Supplies

Medicine and first aid is a big part of any bug out bag. You need to be able to disinfect and dress wounds effectively so that the risk of infection is as low as possible. An infected wound could turn nasty quickly and with no professional medical attention, could turn into a very serious problem.

So you will want to keep antiseptic fluid or wipes, sterile dressings, bandages and tape. You can just buy a standard first aid kit or you can make your own. If you buy a readymade kit and it doesn't have a mirror, you should add one. If you get a cut on your face or back for example, you need to have a mirror to effectively examine and treat it. You should also throw some pain killers in there in case you need them.

Lighting

Lighting is also important, so I would recommend getting a good quality tactical LED flashlight to keep in your bag. Having a portable, instant form of light is invaluable. It's a good idea to also have a backup wind up light to use if you run out of batteries for your main flashlight or to use when you don't need as much illumination.

Communication

You should keep a radio in your bag, preferably wind up, so that you can keep up to date with radio broadcasts that may affect you. I would also recommend having a few snares and a NATO fishing kit so that you can feed yourself more effectively in a bug out situation.

It's slo a good idea to keep a couple of pairs of spare cotton socks and some spare underwear in your bag as sanitation will be a concern. Similarly you should keep a toothbrush and tooth paste. A travel towel will also be very handy. One other thing that can be easily overlooked is toilet roll. You don't want to have to wipe with a pine cone! You can get toilet paper tabs that are very compact and expand when wet saving you room in your bag.

EDC – Everyday Carry

An EDC is a set of items, unique to you, that you carry with you whenever you leave the house. This can be in the form of a small pouch or tin that you keep in your pocket or in the form of something like a survival keychain. Almost all Preppers will have some form of EDC that they will keep with them at all times.

Personally I have an EDC keychain with a few items on it that I use very frequently. I also keep a couple of small self-defense items on me at all times as part of my EDC that I will go into more in the next chapter. For now I'm just going to talk about general EDC items.

The purpose of an EDC is to ensure that you are prepared for unforeseen circumstances at all times. For example, if a disaster strikes when you're out and you can't get home straight away, you may have to spend a day or two fending for yourself.

Multitool

It's completely up to you what you carry with you, but there are a few items you should consider carrying at all times. The first is a multitool. You can get a very small multitool such as the Leatherman Micra. If you don't want to carry a blade on you, or if your local laws don't allow it then you can carry something like the Leatherman Style instead. Both are very small and easy to carry around, yet they have a whole range of functions.

Fire Lighting

You should always have a couple of ways of lighting fire with you. The obvious answer is to carry a lighter. The Firestash by True Utility is a very good option for an EDC lighter. As a backup you can also carry a Ferro rod such as the Bear Grylls Compact Fire Starter as part of your keychain or add a Fresnel lens to your wallet. You can get credit card sized Fresnel Lenses that work exactly the same as a magnifying glass. You can also easily keep some disinfectant swabs in your wallet along with some form of bandage very easily.

Shelter Building

As for shelter building, I wear a paracord bracelet so that I always have cordage on me and I keep a space blanket in my EDC pouch so I will have something to keep the rain off of my head or to keep me warm if I get caught short anywhere.

There are a whole host of other items that you can consider keeping with you such as tweezers (very useful) and a mini compass and much more. Far too much to go into in this chapter at least! If you did want to find out more about creating the best EDC possible and more products that I would recommend, you can take a look at my book dedicated to EDCs.

Self-Defense and Weapons

I carry two self-defense items on me at all times. I'm wouldn't personally feel comfortable carrying anything with me that uses lethal force on a daily basis, even if the area I live in didn't ban carrying anything like this anyway.

The items I carry are a criminal identifier spray called FARB Spray and a monkey fist. This provides me with a short distance ranged deterrent and therefore offers me standoff capabilities. This enables me to point it at any potential attackers and make them think twice before engaging me. They monkey fist, which is essentially a large ball bearing wrapped in paracord, offers me a non-lethal blunt force weapon that also extends my reach and increases the amount of power in the blow. This makes a great combination that I would highly recommend.

There are some other good options for self-defense items too such as the Vipertek VTS-195 which looks like a standard tactical flash light. The difference is that it has a built in stun gun. The noise alone and the shock factor of having a stun gun in your torch will be enough to put off many attackers. This is something that you could keep on your glove box for example. Good quality tactical flashlights can also be used as a blunt force weapon so they're a surprisingly good addition to your self-defense arsenal.

If you do choose to carry a firearm or a knife that can be used for combat then that's entirely up to you as long as you're allowed to by law in whatever part of the world you're in. I personally think there is other items like the first two that I mentioned that are ideal for carrying with you on a day to day basis.

Communication

The last thing I want to cover in this beginners guide to Prepping is the topic of communicating with other people when the phone lines and internet goes down.

Staying in touch with other people will be essential if you want to have the best chance of surviving as possible. This will enable you to find out exactly what's going on in other parts of the world and if there are any safe places that you can travel too. You can also contact others for help if you need to. Being able to communicate with other survivors will be a huge morale boost too, particularly if you end up on your own.

Standard Radio

The most likely form of long distance communication when other conventional forms of communication have failed is radio. Having a standard AM/FM radio will allow you to scan the airways for any emergency broadcasts or messages that may provide valuable information. This could be information on where to go if you need help, they may give you a better idea of what's going on elsewhere, etc.

Communicating Via Radio

If you want to communicate back and forth however, we need to use a different type of radio. There are a few different types of radio that people may use but the most likely is Shortwave. Shortwave radio waves can travel around the curvature of the earth and enable you to communicate over vast distances. You can even communicate with other countries.

So I would recommend taking a look into Shortwave radios and potentially investing in one if you want a sure fire way of communicating with other survivors. However, while you're just starting out, an AM/FM survival radio will do just fine until you want to get more advanced.

Thanks For Reading!

I sincerely hope you enjoyed this book and gained some useful information along the way.

If you want to stay up to date with my regular free book promotions and to also find out about my future releases you can sign up to my mailing list at - www.southshorepublications.com/steverayder

If you would also consider taking the time to leave me an honest review on this book on Amazon I would be extremely appreciative of your feedback.

You can find links to all of my previous books on my author profile at http://www.amazon.com/Steve-Rayder/e/B00U0U3Z3E/ or by searching for "Steve Rayder" on Amazon.

Thanks for reading and I hopefully speak to you all in the next book!